LIBERATING CONCENTRATION CAMP

A PERSONAL ACCOUNT

by (former) Lt-Colonel Leonard Berney R.A. T.D.

Edited by John Wood

Copyright © 2015 Leonard Berney

All rights reserved. This book or any portion thereof may not be reproduced or used in any manner whatsoever without the express written consent of the author except for the use of brief quotations in a book review.

Photos copyright © as noted in captions. Where a photo is labelled 'Source unknown' we have made every reasonable effort to find its copyright holder but without success. If there is in fact a copyright holder of the photo, the editor may be contacted on johnalexwood@gmail.com

ISBN-13: 978-1511541701

ISBN-10: 1511541709

Edited by John Wood

Design and Production by Rosalyn Newhouse

Cover Design by Gemma Harris

Table of Contents

Foreword (Konig) i
Foreword (Eeles) iii
Acknowledgments v
Introduction vii

Chapter 1
   The Liberation of Bergen-Belsen Concentration Camp 1

Chapter 2
   The Rescue Operation 6

Chapter 3
   Water 11

Chapter 4
   Food 12

Chapter 5
   Burials 14

Chapter 6
   The Panzer Barracks 16

Chapter 7
   Creating the 15,000-Bed Hospital 18

Chapter 8
   Evacuating the Concentration Camp 20

Chapter 9
   The Transit and Rehabilitation Camp 22

Chapter 10
   The Belsen Displaced Persons Camp 25

Chapter 11
   Burning Down the Concentration Camp 28

Chapter 12
   The Belsen War Crimes Trial 29

Chapter 13
   Questions I Am Often Asked 30

Chapter 14
    Denying the Denyers 34
UK Media Coverage of the War Crimes Trial 36
Photographs 39
About the Author 107
Appendix
    British Army Units Deployed in the Liberation and
    Rescue Operation 109

Photographs

Figure 1. German officers deliver an important message 40
Figure 2. No-Fire Zone 41
Figure 3. Agreement signed 42
Figure 4. Aerial photo of the camp 43
Figure 5. Entering the No-Fire Zone 44
Figure 6. Commandant Joseph Kramer 45
Figure 7. Male guards lined up 46
Figure 8. Female guards lined up 47
Figure 9. A view of the camp 48
Figure 10. A view of one of the perimeter fences 49
Figure 11. The prisoners lined the sides of the road 50
Figure 12. 'You are safe now. The Germans have gone.' 51
Figure 13. Barbed wire enclosures of the camp 52
Figure 14. A pile of corpses 53
Figure 15. Live prisoners amongst the corpses 54
Figure 16. Hundreds of corpses amongst the trees 55
Figure 17. A large burial pit 56
Figure 18. The SS are arrested 57
Figure 19. British Army units arrive 58
Figure 20. Men's huts 59
Figure 21. Women's huts 60
Figure 22. A hut with no bunks 61
Figure 23. Overcrowded huts 62
Figure 24. Prisoners in a corridor 63
Figure 25. Women's Tented Camp 64
Figure 26. Prisoners wandering about aimlessly 65
Figure 27. A starving prisoner 66
Figure 28. A very ill prisoner 66
Figure 29. A soldier talking to a prisoner 67

Figure 30. A female prisoner kisses soldier's hand 67
Figure 31. Some of the children prisoners 68
Figure 32. Two young girls 68
Figure 33. Boy walks past corpses 69
Figure 34. Women carrying a corpse 70
Figure 35. Inmates dragging a corpse 71
Figure 36. More corpses in their hundreds 72
Figure 37. One of the open water tanks 73
Figure 38. A water cart 74
Figure 39. Water pumps installed 75
Figure 40. A food truck arrives 76
Figure 41. Prisoners distributing food 77
Figure 42. SS guards taking a corpse to the truck 78
Figure 43. Corpses being loaded onto the truck 79
Figure 44. Corpses being offloaded from the truck 80
Figure 45. SS guards dropping a corpse into a burial pit 81
Figure 46. Women SS guards offloading corpses 82
Figure 47. Women SS guards offloading corpses 82
Figure 48. Women SS guards dropping corpses into a burial pit 83
Figure 49. A bulldozer pushing corpses into a burial pit 84
Figure 50. Local dignatories witnessing the burials 85
Figure 51. Prayers being said 86
Figure 52. Grave No 2: Here lies 5,000 86
Figure 53. Entrance to the Panzer Barracks 87
Figure 54. The Panzer Barracks 88
Figure 55. The Barracks Hospital 89
Figure 56. Doctors of the Royal Army Medical Corps 90
Figure 57. Stretcher bearers 91
Figure 58. The 'human laundry' 92

Figure 59. A prisoner being washed and de-loused..... 92
Figure 60. Hospital beds 93
Figure 61. Inside one of the hospital wards 94
Figure 62. Inside one of the hospital wards................. 94
Figure 63. Transit and Rehabilitation part of the
    Barracks 95
Figure 64. A recovering prisoner 95
Figure 65. Prisoners evacuating the camp................... 96
Figure 66. Ex-prisoners taking a warm shower........... 97
Figure 67. An inmate being dusted with DDT 98
Figure 68. Ex-prisoners being helped into a truck...... 99
Figure 69. Inmates being fed 100
Figure 70. Inmates being clothed 101
Figure 71. Many of the children were orphans 102
Figure 72. A school for the children........................... 103
Figure 73. The camp is burned down......................... 104
Figure 74. Belsen notice board.................................... 105
Figure 75. The Belsen Trials.. 106

Leonard Berney aged 18... 108

Foreword

by Nanette Blitz Konig

It is my pleasure to pay tribute and express my gratitude to the courage and valour of the British troops that entered Bergen-Belsen Concentration Camp on 15th April 1945. They were there to fight a war and found horror never before seen. Undoubtedly they were traumatized for life by what they found and had no precedent to guide them how to tackle the indescribable situation with which they were faced. They rose nobly to the task and improvised solutions as best they could which saved many thousands of lives, including mine.

Lt-Colonel L. Berney describes in his book in detail what was found and what was done. I remember him sitting at a table when I approached him and asked if he could write to my family in England to advise them that I had survived. He was kind enough to do this not only once, but one more time to advise them about my situation. These letters are still in my possession.

Occasionally I helped him to communicate with other former prisoners as an interpreter because I spoke Dutch, German and English. As I was the sole survivor of my immediate family, it was his intention to send me to England to my family there, but this proved impossible.

After the war, he came to see me when I was living in London because he wanted to know whether he had achieved his objective for me to join my family.

I strongly believe that the actions of Lt-Colonel L. Berney at Bergen-Belsen contributed to saving my life. Had it not been for his personal intervention, I would probably not have survived. The fact that he was able to help me in this way—among the tens of thousands of prisoners being attended to and amidst this absolutely horrendous overwhelming situation which no normal person can ever understand—was an act far beyond the call of duty.

Nanette Blitz Konig
Belsen Survivor
January 2015

Nanette Blitz Konig is a former classmate of Anne Frank, whom she also met during their time at Bergen-Belsen. 'I don't know how we recognised each other as we were both skeletons.' She now gives talks all over the world about being a survivor of the concentration camp and about the Holocaust and its relevance to modern times.

Foreword
by Major General Nicholas Eeles CBE

Nobody who has watched the film footage of the liberation of Bergen-Belsen concentration camp can have any doubt of the barbarity of the Nazi regime which treated human life with such disdain. The scenes which greeted the liberators were genuinely hellish and the human catastrophe they had to cope with is all but unimaginable to us today.

Lieutenant Colonel Berney has written a short, moving account of his experiences as he sought to save the starving and the sick, and then to rehabilitate and repatriate the survivors. It is a testament to him that the story of the liberation of the camp is told so lucidly and without emotion. It is a testimony which provides further evidence, if any were needed, of the inhumanity of the SS guards, well fed and without apparent guilt or shame, who presided over the avoidable starvation of tens of thousands of prisoners at Bergen-Belsen.

A great many British Army soldiers worked with enormous courage and fortitude to care for the survivors of this notorious concentration camp. They will have lived out their lives deeply affected by that experience, and it is right that we should reflect on their sacrifice at the same time as remembering the millions who lost their lives in the death and concentration camps run by the Nazis.

Major-General Nicholas Eeles CBE
General Officer Commanding Scotland
Chairman, Royal Artillery Historical Trust
March, 2015

Nicholas Eeles has had a long and distinguished career in the British Army having served in Bosnia, Northern Ireland, Germany, Kosovo and Iraq.

Acknowledgments

I would like to thank the Imperial War Museums for helping me source the best possible photos from their extensive Belsen Collection to illustrate this account of the camp's liberation; Gemma Harris for the countless hours of research and help she gave me in compiling the photos and for her superb cover design skills; Rosalyn Newhouse for her invaluable advice (as I have never edited a book before) and for designing the book; Elizabeth Kahn, the daughter of Belsen survivor Nanette Blitz Konig, for inspiring and motivating me to ensure this atrocious story be told in a way that will resonate with people forever; Nanette Blitz Konig and Major General Nicholas Eeles for kindly agreeing to write a foreword; film director Joshua Oppenheimer for kindly agreeing to write the introduction; and my father, Leonard Berney, for bravely recording his account to ensure future generations know, first-hand, what really happened at Belsen. His actions during the four months he was stationed there as its Commandant (together with the rest of the liberating forces) saved many thousands of lives and I will forever be extremely proud of him.

John Wood
Editor

Introduction

A letter from Joshua Oppenheimer

Dear Leonard,

I wept through much of your account of the liberation of Bergen-Belsen. Minutes after I reached the end, I felt the urge to start again from the beginning. I understood then why your writing made such an impact on me. I have known about the Holocaust for as long as I can remember, yet through your account we experience what it was like to encounter the Holocaust for the first time—the moment on 15th April when you walked into an evil that you never before imagined possible. When I rushed back to the beginning, I realised I was grieving that tragic loss of innocence, mourning for a world in which human beings had not yet imagined such horrors. By describing the final moments before you discovered that such evil exists, and by describing the collapse of that illusion, you led me to grieve the fact that a world without genocide is, for now, a fantasy—and this only strengthened my conviction that we must fight fiercely our impulse to look away and forget.

I was equally moved by your and your fellow soldiers' response to this evil: practical, decent, humane—in such sharp contrast to the horror itself. Reading of the months of intense effort restoring the prisoners' health and dignity, I felt humbled. And when you remark that this vision of hell was ultimately transformed into something resembling a holiday camp (alongside the image of the young children attending school at the Displaced Persons camp), I felt nothing short of awe.

Your work at Bergen-Belsen exemplifies the best of

humanity, where moments before the worst prevailed.

In short, thank you for sending me this text. Thank you for the kindness and effort that healed, restored dignity and saved tens of thousands of lives. Thank you for bearing witness.

Joshua Oppenheimer
Oscar®-nominated Film Director
March, 2015

Joshua Oppenheimer is a film director whose work includes The Act of Killing *and* The Look of Silence, *both of which document the genocide that took place during the Indonesian killings of 1965–66.*

Chapter 1

The Liberation of Bergen-Belsen Concentration Camp

In June 1944 the British, American and Canadian armies invaded Normandy and in the following months forced the German Army out of German-occupied France, then Belgium and then Holland. By April 1945 the British Army had entered Germany itself and had crossed the river Rhine, heading for Berlin. On 12th April 1945 we had just crossed the Aller River, some 200 miles into Germany; but the German Army was still putting up a fierce resistance. On that day a Lt-Colonel Schmidt and another German Army officer appeared in front of our front line waving a white flag. They were allowed to approach; our troops thought they were wanting to surrender, but they said no, they were not surrendering, they had been sent by their commanding officer to deliver an important message to our commanding officer. They were blindfolded and brought to the headquarters of the British Army's XIII Corps just outside the town of Winsen. They were escorted to the Corps Commander's caravan and met with Lt-General Brian Horrocks, the Corps Commander.

Schmidt said that he had been sent by the commanding officer of the troops facing us with a proposal. He said that we (the British) were about 12 miles from a civilian detention camp called Bergen-Belsen that contained 60,000 detainees, their German guards and a regiment of Hungarian soldiers guarding the camp perimeter. Typhus had broken out in the camp and his (Schmidt's) commanding officer feared that if a battle were to be fought around that camp, the prisoners would escape and spread the disease to the surrounding German civilian population and more than likely, to the British soldiers too.

The proposal was this: The area around the camp should not be fought over, a 'No-Fire Zone' around it should be established, the British would not fire into this zone, and the Germans would not fire from it or defend it. The British would take control of this detention camp in an orderly manner. Once we had taken over the camp the German Army military units in the Zone and the detention centre's guards would withdraw east, behind their side of the Zone. The British would gain the area of the Zone without resistance from the Germans. The Hungarians would become our prisoners of war. Schmidt produced a map with the proposed No-Fire Zone of about 5 by 3½ miles marked on it.[*]

Although this was a most unusual proposal, Lt-General Horrocks saw the sense to it and a document setting out the terms was typed out and signed by both parties. The German officers were blindfolded again and transported back to their own lines.

Later, we obtained an RAF aerial photo of this camp, but it did not, of course, give any clue as to the conditions inside the camp.

It was not until three days later, 15th April, that our

---

[*] A few days later, when Hitler heard what the German Army Commander (a Colonel Harries) had arranged, Harries was summoned to Berlin, tried for treason for ceding territory to the enemy without resistance, and executed.

Liberating Belsen Concentration Camp

advance units reached the edge of the No-Fire Zone. At that time, I was a member of the General Staff of XIII Corps, rank of Major. On that day, I was told by our Chief of Staff to take a jeep and a driver and rendezvous at the detention centre with Lt-Colonel Taylor, the Commanding Officer of 63rd Anti-Tank Regiment, who had been given the job of entering the Zone and taking charge of the camp. I was to come back to Corps HQ as soon as possible to give the Chief of Staff and the Corps Commander a report of the situation in the camp.

On the way to the camp I recall being apprehensive, to say the least. My driver and I were way in front of our front line, in enemy territory. Was it a trap? In the event, the German soldiers we passed did hold their fire and we got to the camp entrance unhindered. I noticed that the Germans had placed 'Danger Typhus' notices at the entrances to the Zone. I arrived at the camp entrance just as Lt-Colonel Taylor and his advance party of about fifty men arrived.

About sixty camp guards, about half of them women, with the Camp Commandant Joseph Kramer at their head, had lined up on the road outside the camp. They were members of the *Schutzstaffeln* (SS), the German internal security organization responsible for, among other things, controlling detention centres. (We later learned that there had been some 300 SS personnel at the camp but most had fled when they heard about the take-over arrangement.) Kramer had some hand-over documents ready for Lt-Colonel Taylor to sign. He told us there were about 60,000 inmates in the camp, of whom he estimated some 10,000 were dead but unburied, and that the death rate was running at about 500 a day. He said that there had been no water or food in the camp for several days.

Nearby at the side of the road were several hundred German soldiers, with their rifles, waiting for the order to move out, as agreed in the No-Fire Zone document. It was a weird situation. For months we had been in mortal combat with the German Army, and here I was, surrounded by them, all fully armed, hoping that they would keep to the no-fire arrangement. Fortunately for me and the others in the advance party, there were no 'incidents'.

While we were talking to Kramer, we heard shooting coming from the camp. (We could not see into the camp from where we were.) Kramer explained that some of the prisoners were rioting and trying to raid the food stores and that the guards he had left in the camp were having to open fire to keep order. Taylor decided to enter the camp to investigate. Taylor, Kramer and I together with the Intelligence officer (a Lieutenant Sington), who had arrived with his loud-hailer van, and two army photographers drove into the camp. We drove the length of the camp and back It was nearly half a mile long. Announcements were made in German and other languages that the British Army had arrived to take over the camp; the inmates were now safe but had to stay where they were.

As we drove along the camp's main road we saw dead bodies lying beside the road, and many hundreds of emaciated men and women prisoners still mostly behind barbed wire. We saw many long wooden huts with corpses littering the ground between them. In open areas at the rear of the huts, more piles of corpses. At the end of the road, we saw a large open mass grave containing hundreds of corpses. The sights, the stench, the sheer horror of the place, were indescribable.

After fighting our way from Normandy for the last ten months, we were used to seeing battle casualties, but we had no warning of what were about to see. I had never experienced anything remotely like it before. I remember being completely shattered. We did not go into any of the huts—that was a horror to come.

After this brief tour, we returned to the camp entrance and Taylor ordered his men to arrest Kramer and to disarm all the SS personnel and to place them under guard in their quarters.

Taylor then wrote a report, which I took back to Corps HQ. It was night-time before I got there. I described to General Horrocks as best I could the huge humanitarian disaster that Belsen camp was. From Taylor's written and my verbal report the General realized the urgency; Belsen was our responsibility now. He and his staff worked through the night to organize the help that was so clearly essential. They sent out orders to round up all the food stores, water trucks and army medical services they could get hold of quickly.

The great Belsen rescue effort had started.

Chapter 2

The Rescue Operation

The next morning, 16th April, I was told by the Chief of Staff that I was to return to the camp and join 224 Military Government Detachment* that had been sent there to help coordinate the work of the military units assigned to the camp. I found Major Miles, the officer in charge of that unit. He told me to look around the camp and acquaint myself with the size of the problem. Little did I know it but I was to be working in that camp and with its survivors for the next four months.

I looked inside several of the huts and some dilapidated tents that had been erected as 'overflow' accommodation. No words of mine can even come close to describing the ghastly conditions in those huts. What I saw there I will never forget.

The huts were intended to house perhaps 100; most had over 500 in them. The conditions were beyond appalling, especially since nearly all the inmates were desperately ill with emaciation, typhus, dysentery, diarrhoea and tuberculosis. The bunks in the huts each had three and sometimes four occupants. Some prisoners were lying on the floor as they had no other place to lie. Some of the bunks contained corpses. In some huts there were no bunks and in some, the occupants were so packed in,

---

* Military Government Detachments were formed as the Allies entered German territory. Their purpose was to take control of the German civil administration in areas occupied by Allied forces. They were staffed by officers and men seconded from their combat units who had experience of civil administration.

there was not enough room for them to lie down. The stench in those huts was overwhelming.

There were no washing facilities in the huts. The latrines were just trenches between the huts, and many of the prisoners in the huts were too weak to go outside and use them. Clearly many had lost all self-respect and hope. In other areas, the inmates had left their huts and were huddled in small groups or were wandering about aimlessly. Outside and at the back of the huts, corpses in various stages of decomposition were everywhere. The excreta-laden dust blowing round the camp was a serious medical threat. I was nauseated and horrified. The whole scene was a veritable Dante's Inferno.

I found that Bergen-Belsen camp was divided into several sections. There was a 'Specials' section with Jewish inmates who held passports of various foreign countries. A 'Neutrals' section held foreign nationals who had been trapped in Germany at the outbreak of war. The 'Star', or 'Exchange' camp contained 'Exchange Jews', including several hundred children, nationals of countries occupied by Germany being held ready to exchange for German citizens who were interned by the Allies. There was a 'Hungarian Camp' with Jews from Hungary. The 'Recuperation Camp' contained slave workers from other camps who had become too sick to work; however, there were in fact no medical facilities there. Then there was the tented 'Women's Camp' with more sick prisoners, and a 'Small Women's Camp', also tented, used as an overflow of the Women's Camp.

About two-thirds of the prisoners were women, one-third were men. There were 400 to 500 children. Crowded into, and dying, in Bergen-Belsen were people from every walk of life: academics, professionals, musicians, political activists, housewives, doctors, teachers, skilled factory workers, clerks, convicted criminals, anyone the Nazi regime classed as 'undesirable'. Half or more were Jewish, there just because they were Jews. Some prisoners were in rags, some were in blue-and-white striped pyjama-like prison clothes, some recent arrivals and 'exchange' prisoners were in normal street clothes. They were of many nationalities, speaking many different languages. Some were at the depths of degradation, had lost all sense of normality. Men and women were relieving themselves in plain view. The majority were clearly very ill and emaciated, some others, recent arrivals, were in fairly good health.

At the end of 1944 the camp had held about 15,000 prisoners. Although it was full, life was harsh but just about tolerable. At that time, in 1944, the Soviet Army started sweeping through the German-occupied area of Russia and Poland. In front of the Russians there were many slave labour camps and 'Final Solution' death camps (gas chambers). Hitler gave an order that none of the prisoners were to fall into the Russian Army's hands and that all the prisoners and their guards were to be evacuated west into Germany itself and placed in camps there. This resulted in the 'death marches' of that winter of 1944/5. Many hundreds of thousands of prisoners—it is said, more than half of them—died on the journey. Belsen was one of those designated camps and from early in 1945 hundreds, sometimes thousands, of starved, sick and dying prisoners arrived daily.

On that second day, 16th April, officers and men of the units ordered to the camp started to arrive and were

LIBERATING BELSEN CONCENTRATION CAMP

reconnoitring the area. Gradually the extent of the horror was becoming clear. Brigadier Glynn-Hughes, the senior medical officer of the British Army, had arrived and had taken overall command of the camp. That evening he called a meeting of officers to receive reports on what they had found. What was needed, he said, was A PLAN. But what should you do when faced with 60,000 dead, sick and dying people? We were in the army to fight a war and to beat the enemy. We were good at that, having been in combat for the last ten months, but none of us had any experience of dealing with the situation in Belsen and we were all more or less traumatized by the sights we had seen. I myself, although a 'senior officer', had turned 25 years of age only a few days before. Most of the men sent to deal with that human disaster were in their late teens or early twenties, even younger than I was. What we suddenly found ourselves faced with was beyond anyone's comprehension.

Our major priority, Glynn-Hughes said, was to save lives, or as many lives as possible. He set out several immediate tasks:

- Provision of water and food
- Burial of the dead
- Evacuation of the camp
- Hospitalization of the sick
- Rehabilitation of the fit

Setting up medical facilities within the concentration camp itself was considered, but it was decided that the whole area was so infested with disease that to attempt this would be a waste of the limited medical facilities we had. Where to, and how to, evacuate those tens of thousands of inmates was left as an open question. Tasks were detailed out to various officers: I was detailed to organize the water supply.

Chapter 3

Water

The situation I faced was that the camp's water supply had broken down four days prior; the mains electricity to the camp had been cut.

The only source of water in the camp was two fairly large open-air reservoirs next to the road through the camp that I believe were meant for fire-fighting purposes. The water in them was absolutely foul; there was miscellaneous rubbish floating in them. Nevertheless, out of desperation, inmates were scooping up some of that water in their rusty utensils.

Corps HQ had ordered the Royal Army Service Corps to immediately spare as many of their water bowsers as they could and several arrived during the day. I set up half a dozen water distribution points where the inmates could draw water from the bowsers. I was also allocated twenty or so soldiers that I placed at these water points to help the weaker inmates and to prevent mobbing. We had the bowsers being emptied and refilled and emptied again till dark. That 'drill' went on from dawn to dusk for the next two or three days.

We heard that the Civilian Fire Service in the nearby town of Celle had some portable pumps. Some of the firemen and their pumps were quickly brought to the camp and we started drawing water from a stream that ran along one edge of the camp. Then an army engineering unit arrived; by the end of the third day they had restored the camp's water system—from then on there was no shortage of water.

Leonard Berney

Chapter 4
Food

On the day after liberation, Royal Army Service Corps trucks arrived loaded with army Compo* packs, together with several army cooks. They quickly got the boilers in the two main cookhouses going and prepared a stew from the contents of the Compo packs: tinned beef, tinned pork, bacon, sausages and thick soup. The packs also contained some cheese and hard biscuits.

There had been no food in the camp for several days† and distributing the stew to many thousands of starving and desperate inmates and controlling the crowds was a problem. We had nowhere nearly enough soldiers to take this food to each hut and we had to rely on the system the Germans had used. Inmates from each hut had to come to the cookhouse and collect bin-loads to carry back to their huts. Once in the huts, the Hut Leader (*Capo*) was responsible for sharing out the food fairly. Once the German guards had gone, the food distribution system broke down. The *Capos* fled or hid. Several were murdered by the inmates of their hut in reprisal for the brutal treatment they had received at the hands of their *Capo*. Collection teams did not come to the cookhouse; instead it was 'every man/woman for him/her self.' The fitter of the inmates came to collect food for themselves—

---

* Compo: Composite Rations

† Later, a large number of Red Cross parcels that had originated from Hungary were discovered in one of the huts of the SS quarters. Some had been opened and the contents presumably consumed by the SS guards.

many of the sick people in the huts received nothing.

Another problem concerned the food itself. Many who were emaciated and starving bolted down this rich food and that sadly caused their deaths. It was estimated that 1,500 to 2,000 died because of the food we gave them. But who, given the circumstances we faced, could have foreseen that? We compensated with the thought that those poor people were so near death that, whether we had fed them or not, they probably would have died anyway.

Chapter 5

Burials

The camp was provided with two incinerators which were able to cope with the deaths of prisoners that occurred in the period up to the end of 1944. In 1945 the number of deaths had increased to such an extent that these incinerators could not cope. The SS then arranged prisoners' corpses into piles interlaced with wood, doused the funeral pyre with petrol and attempted to incinerate the corpses that way. The smell caused complaints from the local population and that plan was abandoned. The SS then had the prisoners dig a large burial pit at the end of the camp and corpses were taken up there and thrown in. In the last weeks before liberation, the death rate had reached several hundred every day and that method broke down too. It seems that those corpses that could not be carried to the pit were just piled up in the areas at the rear of the huts.

With many thousands of decomposing corpses lying unburied, it was a medical necessity (threat of cholera) to bury them as soon as possible. We had no option but to continue what the Germans had started, to bury the corpses in mass graves. A Royal Engineer bulldozer was trucked in to dig more deep pits. It was decided to use the SS guards, both male and female, to remove the corpses from the camp area and carry them up to the burial pits. In some places, the piles of remains were so decomposed that they could not be handled. Pits had to be dug next to the piles and the bulldozer simply pushed the corpses into the pit. Imagine the thoughts of the two young soldiers who took it in turns to drive the bulldozer! The SS were forced to transport those dead prisoners from morning to night—this was watched every day by the former prisoners. There was much jeering and expression of hatred.

It took about two weeks before the backlog had been buried and the daily burials were those who had died the previous night. In the end, some ten mass graves were required. Sign boards were erected: '5000 buried here', '3000 buried here' etcetera.

So that the German civilians could not in the future say 'it never happened,' during these burials, we brought the mayors and other prominent civilians from miles around the camp to the burial sites to witness for themselves what their countrymen had perpetrated on innocent people. In addition, army photographers recorded the horrifying scenes for future generations.

Soon, many British reporters and press photographers and newsreel cameramen came to the camp and 'Belsen, the horror camp' was widely reported in the UK. Public reaction was shock and outrage. Ironically, it was the story and photographs of Belsen that for the first time, even after five years of war, made the people of Britain realize the atrocities the Nazi regime had practiced.

When the burials were completed, the SS men and women were imprisoned in the jail at the nearby town of Celle to await a war crimes trial.

Chapter 6

The Panzer Barracks

After having organized the water supply, the next job I was given was to scour the countryside to find what food stocks there might be that we could requisition. We knew there was a German Army barracks 2 miles up the road from the concentration camp. I found there a very large military barracks. (The German Army had left several days prior.) The barracks was a Panzer (tank) training school designed for 20,000 soldiers. There were dozens of two-story dormitory buildings, fully equipped with beds and bedding, dining halls and lecture rooms. There was a 200-bed hospital still with its staff and medical supplies.

I found the food store of the barracks holding hundreds of tons of various foodstuffs, tinned meat, powdered milk, vegetables, sugar, cocoa, potatoes and so forth. I also found there a large bakery capable of baking 60,000 loaves a day, complete with many tons of flour. The civilian staff was still there. On the way back to the concentration camp I discovered in the nearby village of Belsen a sizeable cooperative dairy that had been supplying the area with milk, butter and cheese.

I reported the food stocks I had found to Major Miles of Military Government, and also that the modern empty barracks was, in my opinion, ideal to be converted into a hospital and recuperation camp. He arranged with the officers of the Royal Artillery Regiment posted to the camp to immediately requisition the whole of the Panzer

Barracks together with its food stores and hospital, and also to requisition the dairy in the village of Belsen.

Chapter 7

Creating the 15,000-Bed Hospital

A British Army field hospital, an Army Field Ambulance Unit and two Casualty Clearing Units had been taken out of the line and ordered to Belsen. They began converting about half of the Panzer Barracks into a vast hospital. Halls and dormitories were turned into hospital wards. Military Government gave orders to the mayors of the towns and villages surrounding the camp that all homes, shops and clinics were to hand over all spare beds, blankets, medicines, surgical equipment and men's and women's clothing. These were collected in the Regiment's trucks. Other men from the Regiment rounded up all the civilian German nurses and doctors they could find and brought them to work at the hospital we were creating in the Panzer Barracks. In addition, German Army doctors held in our prisoner-of-war camps were collected and brought to Belsen.

Typhus is carried by lice; the great fear was of bringing typhus from the concentration camp into the new hospital we were creating. A 'human laundry' was set up in the stables of the barracks—when the sick inmates arrived at the hospital, they were to be thoroughly washed and deloused before entering the wards. This 'human laundry' would be staffed by German Army doctors and nurses transferred from the original Panzer Barracks hospital, working under British Army supervision.

On 21st April, six days after liberation, the newly created hospital was ready to receive its first patients from the concentration camp. A remarkable achievement! The records show that by the time the concentration camp was emptied, between 14,000 and 15,000 patients were admitted and treated there—the largest hospital in the world, before or since!

Chapter 8

Evacuating the Concentration Camp

As soon as the hospital was ready, we started to evacuate the inmates from the concentration camp. Doctors from the Army Medical units went into each hut and with a very cursory examination, decided which of the sick would be taken to hospital (they marked their foreheads with a cross) and which were so ill that they were beyond saving and would be left to die. The ones to be saved were then stripped of all their clothing, wrapped in a blanket and stretchered out of the huts and ambulanced up to the new hospital.

About two weeks after liberation, ninety-seven medical students (all in their early twenties) arrived from the UK and were allocated one or two to each hut. They greatly helped the problem of feeding those too sick to feed themselves.

While the hospital was being created, other soldiers were given the task of converting the remainder of the Panzer Barracks buildings into a vast Transit and Rehabilitation Camp. The fit (the definition of 'fit' was any ex-prisoner who could walk) would be conveyed to the Transit and Rehabilitation Camp to recuperate and, as soon as they were well enough to travel, would then be repatriated to the countries they came from.

Having completed the task of discovering food supplies, I was allotted the job of taking charge of the evacuation of the 25,000 or so 'fit' inmates to the newly prepared Transit and Rehabilitation Camp in the barracks. Allocated to me were about fifty soldiers, an Army Mobile

Shower unit, an Army Disinfestation unit, and about a dozen trucks with their drivers. We also recruited some of the fitter female ex-prisoner inmates to help.

As soon as the Panzer Barracks Transit Camp was ready, evacuation of the so-called fit started. Evacuation was by nationality; the Western Europeans were evacuated first because we knew they would be quickly repatriated from the Transit Camp. Next were Russians and then other nationalities where we knew that repatriation arrangements were ready.

The procedure at the concentration camp was this: First, each ex-prisoner was registered, then given some soap and a towel to take a hot shower. After the shower they were thoroughly sprayed with DDT to kill any lice. Finally, they were helped into the trucks to be ferried to the Transit Camp in the barracks.

There were problems of inmates trying to 'gatecrash' the departing trucks. I had the use of about twenty soldiers to keep order. All of us worked twelve to fourteen hours, 'processing' 1,000 weak and sick people every day. Even at this rate, it took three weeks to empty the camp. This meant that thousands of prisoners had to wait in the old disease-ridden camp for several days until we could evacuate them to safety. The last inmate was evacuated on 19th May.

In this period, every morning those of us who worked in the camp were liberally sprayed with DDT. The medics inoculated us against various diseases. Fortunately, few if any soldiers contracted any disease other than dysentery, which almost all of us had—but we kept on working.

Chapter 9
The Transit and Rehabilitation Camp

Just before the concentration camp was finally cleared, I was given the job of being in charge of the Transit and Rehabilitation Camp in the Panzer Barracks, as the 'Camp Commandant.' By then the Transit Camp received and housed some 25,000 men, women and children in various stages of malnutrition and emaciation, but not ill enough to be hospitalised. The main task that I and the about thirty officers and men allocated to me had was to ensure that all the ex-prisoners had a clean bed and adequate clothing, and were fed, and generally to prepare them for the very long journey home to the countries they had originally been taken from. They were to be accommodated in national and regional groups, men and women separately. We prepared lists of identity details for authorities of the countries involved. There were nationals of no less than forty-one countries in the Transit Camp!

The clothing store, supplied by requisition of clothes and shoes from the surrounding German homes and shops, was dubbed by the British press as the 'Harrods at Belsen'. The cookhouses and general maintenance jobs round the camp were staffed by ex-inmates themselves, under my men's supervision. During May, Red Cross workers started to arrive and were a great help in welfare matters, especially with the children, and in achieving a sense of civilized normality throughout the camp.

The occasional squabbles—mostly about who would have

to stay next to whom, or be separated from whom—and some settling of old concentration camp scores were handled with tact by the British 'Tommies'.

Typhus is contracted from being bitten by infected body lice; the disease takes one to two weeks to incubate. A substantial number of ex-prisoners arriving at the Transit Camp were infected but as yet without symptoms and only got sick after some days in their new surroundings. There was therefore a daily transfer of those new typhus victims from the Transit Camp to the Hospital. At the same time, every day several hundred hospital patients who had recovered and had been discharged were being admitted to the Transit Camp. Additionally, coaches and buses from many countries were continually arriving to take home their now fit-to-travel survivors.

We also had to deal with an ever increasing number of enquiries coming from authorities and relatives worldwide seeking information about individual ex-prisoners. We set up a mailing system for ex-prisoners to mail out postcards to their relatives outside of Germany. Then every day there were visits from politicians and the media that had to be escorted and dealt with. Busy days indeed!

Many of the ex-prisoners who had been kept in the concentration camp for months or even years had become de-humanized. After they were rescued and placed in civilized living conditions, given clean clothing and three decent meals a day, and a proper bed to sleep in, I was surprised and gratified to see how quickly they recovered and became human beings again. One instance illustrates that: after the news about the conditions at Belsen and the state of the survivors reached Britain,

America and several other countries, gift parcels started to arrive. One of these was a crate of hundreds of lipsticks. I said, 'Of all the things these people desperately need, lipstick is certainly not one.' I was wrong! When they were given out to the women survivors, the effect on their morale was extraordinary. Many started to take an interest in their appearance again, to care for their hair and clothing. Morale took a sudden boost!

After two or three weeks, the men ex-prisoners started sprucing themselves up too. One began to see couples arm-in-arm strolling around the barracks. From June onwards there were several weddings. Life for some was returning to normal.

Chapter 10
The Belsen Displaced Persons Camp

The survivors from Belgium, Holland, France and other Allied countries were swiftly repatriated. That left the great majority who had originated from central and eastern Europe, Poland, Ukraine, Russia, Hungary, Yugoslavia etcetera, countries that had by now been occupied by Soviet Union troops. Many ex-prisoners from those countries feared that, as soon as they entered their own now Soviet-occupied countries, they would be arrested and imprisoned again as 'German collaborators and/or spies for the Allies'. Moreover, in the case of the Poles, many of the towns and villages they had come from had been destroyed and obliterated by the war. The result—they refused to be repatriated!

This was a surprise to the British authorities—it had always been assumed that all the ex-prisoners would want to leave the Transit Camp as soon as possible. Thus, after the Western ex-prisoners had gone, we were left with over 20,000 inmates who refused to go home. A new and completely unexpected situation! The same situation faced the authorities in many liberated concentration camps throughout the British and American Control Zones. Eventually those camps were designated 'Displaced Persons (DP) Camps', and the Panzer Barracks Transit and Rehabilitation Camp was renamed 'Belsen DP Camp'.

I came to accept that we were in for a long haul. So I, the soldiers I had, and the less ill of the ex-prisoners themselves set about making life at least tolerable for people stuck in the DP camp. For example: we organized a school for the children; the barracks had a large tented theatre with 800 seats, so we scouted for talent among the inmates and put on a series of concerts; we put on cinema shows; a 'hairdressing salon' was set up and staffed by some Hungarian women. One British newspaper even told its readers that Belsen had been turned into a holiday camp!

By May, the inmates were becoming anxious about their future. The great majority wanted to emigrate to the USA but the Americans refused to give asylum to any DPs from Germany. The DPs' next choice was the UK or France or any other Western European country or Australia or New Zealand. One by one each of those countries, like the USA, refused entry. Anxiety turned to desperation. 'What is going to happen to us? Are we to be kept in DP camps in Germany for the rest of our lives? That is totally unacceptable.'

By June or July, the majority of the inmates still in the camp were Jewish. To these people the solution to their problem, as they saw it perhaps the *only* solution, was to somehow make their way to Palestine to join the Jewish community there. From then on, nearly every day, groups of twenty to fifty would leave Belsen for that very long and perilous journey.

At that time, in 1945, the government of Palestine was the responsibility of the British government under a United Nations mandate. An immigration quota system was in force and the quota for 1945 had already been filled and exceeded. In Palestine a civil war was being fought between the Arabs and the Jews. The Arabs wanted to keep out the Jewish DPs from Germany, while Jewish militia groups were assisting them to arrive. The British military in Palestine were trying to stop any further 'illegal' immigrants from Europe and at the same time trying to keep the Arab and Jewish militias apart. As a result the British were being attacked by both the Jews and the Arabs. I, as Commandant of the Belsen DP Camp, received official orders to do whatever had to be done to prevent Jewish groups from making their way to Palestine. This was an unworkable order—Belsen DP Camp was not a prison and the gates were open. Moreover my sympathies were with 'my' Holocaust survivors. While I could not actively assist those groups leaving the camp, I saw to it that they had sufficient food and water to last several days and I gave them the locations of DP camps in the British and American zones that were on their route south.

At the end of August 1945 I received instructions to hand over control of the camp to the United Nations Relief and Rehabilitation Agency. Belsen DP Camp continued under UNRRA's control until 1950 when it was finally closed down. The camp then became the HQ and base of the British Army of the Rhine (BAOR). It is still in use today by British and NATO forces.

Chapter 11
Burning Down the Concentration Camp

As to the concentration camp itself, by 19th May the last inmate had been evacuated and the decision was made to bring in army flamethrowers and burn down all the more than 100 huts. The last hut was torched on 21st May. A large notice board was erected there.

In all it is estimated that Bergen-Belsen saw the death of at least 50,000 prisoners. Originally built in 1940 for Belgian and Dutch prisoners of war, in 1941 it housed 20,000 Russian POWs. By 1943 almost all of them had died from disease or starvation. Belsen was then designated as a civilian internment camp. Between 1943 and the liberation in April 1945 it is estimated that 17,000 deaths occurred. After liberation there were 13,000 more deaths.

Chapter 12
The Belsen War Crimes Trial

In September 1945 a War Crimes Trial was convened in Lüneburg, not far from Belsen. There were forty-five defendants. The Belsen trial attracted substantial national and international media interest. More than 100 representatives of the news media reported at length on the trial's progress. The press named the camp the 'Horror Camp' and Kramer was 'The Beast of Belsen'. Through the media, not only did the world learn about the thousands of deaths by hunger and disease at Belsen—communicated especially forcefully by the film and photo footage produced by the British Army photographers—but it was at the Belsen trial that for the first time the use of gas chambers for organised mass murder at Auschwitz-Birkenau received a public airing.

One of the main accusations against Kramer and some of the others was that the prisoners were deliberately starved, and that many thousands died of starvation although there were large stores of food available in the Panzer Barracks, only two miles away. I was called to give evidence of my visit to the Barracks and the amount of food stocks I found there.

Eleven of the defendants, including Kramer and three of the female SS guards, were found guilty, mostly of the crimes they committed at Auschwitz, and were hanged. Most of the others were given long gaol sentences. Some were released due to insufficient evidence against them.

Chapter 13

Questions I Am Often Asked

Did Winston Churchill and the British government know about Belsen?

British intelligence knew there were scores of detention camps and slave labour camps in Germany, but knew little of their size or of the conditions in the individual camps. At the beginning of March 1945 a prisoner in Belsen, a Turkish doctor, was released; the ship taking him to Sweden stopped at Liverpool and he was interviewed there. He gave the authorities details of the camp as it was at the end of February. What he could not tell them was the exact location of the camp. It was after he left that the massive overcrowding took place, the typhus epidemic started and the daily deaths increased dramatically. Almost certainly, the British authorities had no detailed knowledge of the conditions in Belsen at the time of its liberation.

Why did not the British not do more to rescue the prisoners?

As explained in the answer to the previous question, we (the troops liberating the camp) had no prior knowledge of the conditions in the concentration camp. In fact we did not know we were approaching a concentration camp until the German colonel came across our lines and told us. He had no information of the conditions inside the camp as he himself had never entered the camp; he only knew that there were 60,000 prisoners and that typhus was rampant.

Remember, also, that at this time the battle against the German Army was still raging. We were in 'hot pursuit' and racing to get to Berlin. Our army, like every army on the advance, was desperately short of men, short of food and water, short of transport, short of ammunition, short of medical backup. Nevertheless, the Corps Commander immediately took many combat and support units out of the line to deal with the completely unexpected catastrophe in the camp.

After the first day, more and more resources were being taken out of the line to aid the rescue operation. (See the Appendix*.) It is said that General Montgomery, the head of the British 21st Army Group, called General Eisenhower, head of the Allied Armies, to say, 'We can either deal with the disaster at Belsen, or we can get on with the war. We can't do both!'

How did it affect me?

I was shattered and nauseated. For the next two or three years I would get 'flashback' visions. Eventually, however, I put that horrendous experience behind me—I had to get on with life.

Did the SS guards show any remorse?

No. One of the main concepts of Nazism was that certain classes of people were not normal humans like the Germans; they were sub-human. The sub-humans included all Jews, Poles, Russians, homosexuals, Jehovah's Witnesses, communists, gypsies and more.

---

* Hostilities ceased on 8th May 1945, three weeks after the liberation. From then on directing more of the needed facilities to the camp became possible.

Those sub-humans had to be eliminated from the Third Reich. They were rounded up and placed in detention camps. The SS were responsible for overseeing those camps.

The guards at Belsen were all hardened SS with long experience at their jobs. They had as much compassion for the prisoners as an abattoir worker has for the animals he slaughters. In their eyes they were doing what they were paid to do, and doing it in the way they were supposed to do it; they were doing nothing wrong.

How did working in the concentration camp affect the young soldiers?

They were, of course, shocked and horrified. What made it possible for them to do what we did was army discipline. All of us at the camp had for many months fought our way through from France and were toughened soldiers. In the army, the man at the top makes a decision, men under him are given orders, you obey those orders—whatever you are told to do, you GET ON WITH IT. That is what happened at Belsen.

In my opinion, the officers and men of the British Army who found themselves pitched into the disaster that was Belsen acquitted themselves outstandingly.

Wouldn't the German civilians living near the camp have known what was happening inside?

I do not believe they did. The camp was situated in the open countryside, well away from the nearest houses. The perimeter fence was patrolled by military. No civilians were allowed near the camp, and never inside. In Nazi Germany you did not ask questions; if you did you might well have become one of the prisoners yourself.

What was the reaction in the UK when the camp was liberated?

From the book *Belsen* by Joanne Reilly: 'The scenes of barbarity relayed from Belsen shocked the world. In Britain, Belsen dominated conversation and the newspaper letter pages. Wireless broadcasts, newspaper reports and newsreels triggered a wave of genuine shock and horror across the whole country. Many have never forgotten the feelings evoked in them on seeing the newsreel footage of Belsen for the first time.'

Although the British had been bombed and deprived for five years, ironically the pictures and stories coming out of Belsen made them aware for the first time 'what the Nazis were really like' and 'what we had been fighting for.'

Were there any gas chambers in Belsen?

No, there were not. Gas chambers were installed at six 'extermination' camps mostly in the East. The death toll at Belsen was caused by starvation and disease.

Did you meet Anne Frank?

No. Anne Frank was a 16-year-old Dutch girl in Belsen. She died there several days before the liberation.

Was there any cannibalism at Belsen?

I personally never saw any signs of cannibalism although several of the prisoners have given evidence that there were a number of instances.

Chapter 14

Denying the Denyers

In 1932 Germany was a Democratic Republic. In a general election in November of that year Adolph Hitler's National Socialist German Workers Party (NAZI) obtained the greatest number of votes. In January of 1933, Hitler and the NAZI party came to power. By the end of that year democracy had been replaced by a dictatorship with Hitler as the Fuhrer.

One of the early results was the establishment throughout Germany of slave labour camps and detention (concentration) camps. Arrested and imprisoned were Jews, Romany, homosexuals, trade unionists and any person suspected of not complying with Nazi ideals. First in Germany, then in Austria and later in the many countries occupied by the Germans. Over the next few years the majority of those prisoners were worked to death, starved to death or deliberately murdered. The number killed is said to be 17 million.

In the last few years I have become aware that there were people in the UK and elsewhere who deny that the Holocaust ever happened; they assert that it is all a lie. It was *not* a lie. I know what Nazism did: I was there!

I have always thought it important to do what I could to inform the younger generation that the Holocaust *did* happen and to remind them of the events of the 1930s and how easily a democratic government can become a dictatorship if the citizens of that country allow that to happen. Over recent years I have written several articles and given lectures and now I present this book about my experience at the Bergen-Belsen Concentration Camp.

UK Media Coverage of the War Crimes Trial

The Belsen War Crimes Trial attracted substantial national and international media interest. More than 100 representatives of the news media reported at length on the trial's progress. The press named the camp the 'Horror Camp' and Kramer was 'The Beast of Belsen'. One of the main accusations against Kramer and some of the others were that the prisoners were deliberately starved and that many thousands died of starvation although there were large stores of food available in the Panzer Barracks, only 2 miles away.

I was called to give evidence of my visit to the Barracks and the amount of food stocks I found there.

Liberating Belsen Concentration Camp

The Star (UK Newspaper)

Thursday, 30th September, 1945

The article reads:

The first witness today was the man who succeeded Kramer as commandant of the camp—25-year-old Major Adolfus Leonard Berney, Royal Artillery, whose home is at Lancaster Gate, London.

He has worked at Belsen since its liberation, and under him it has been transformed into a holiday centre for displaced persons.

Major Berney told the court: "I can see no conceivable reason why the camp should not have been supplied with food by the Germans."

When he went there he found a bakery capable of producing 60,000 loaves a day.

"There appeared to me to be a very vast quantity of material in the bakehouse," he said. "It is working now and most of the staff are the same."

Medical supplies found in the camp were so ample that they had not yet been exhausted.

When the British entered the water was so foul that they brought in fire pumps and pumped water from the river. In about four days good water was available for everyone.

Major Blackhouse, prosecuting officer: Was anything lacking to provide full water, medical and sanitary services?

Major Berney: If the camp administration had wanted supplies these things could have been given.

In the store of a military school three kilometres from the camp he found

600 tons of potatoes, 120 tons of tinned meat, and 30 tons of sugar.

Major Berney was questioned by Mr. Sterling and the President on the procedure under which Kramer obtained supplies.

He replied that he had the impression that a captain had to send quantities on some sort of a ration scale.

Photographs

We are fortunate that British Army photographers recorded the events leading up to the liberation of the Bergen-Belsen Concentration Camp, the conditions inside the camp, rescuing the prisoners and the subsequent care taken of them.

Following are some of their photographs.

Figure 1. On 12th April 1945, Lieutenant-Colonel Schmidt and another German Army officer appeared in front of our front line waving a white flag. They were allowed to approach; our troops thought they were wanting to surrender, but they said they were not surrendering, they had been sent by their commanding officer to deliver an important message to our commanding officer. They were blindfolded and brought to the headquarters of the British Army's XIII Corps. © Imperial War Museums (BU 3624)

Figure 2. The German officers proposed a No-Fire Zone around a civilian detention camp, Bergen-Belsen. This is the map of the No-Fire Zone, an area of about 5 by 3½ miles. The Bergen-Belsen camp is in the center, about 2 miles from Belsen village. Our troops were advancing from the southwest. Source unknown

Figure 3. The two German officers at XIII Corps Headquarters with Lieutenant-Colonel Taylor (far left) who was later detailed to take over the camp from the Germans. The No-Fire Zone was agreed and signed by the Germans and the British. The two German officers were blindfolded again and escorted back to the German lines. ©
Imperial War Museums (BU 4068)

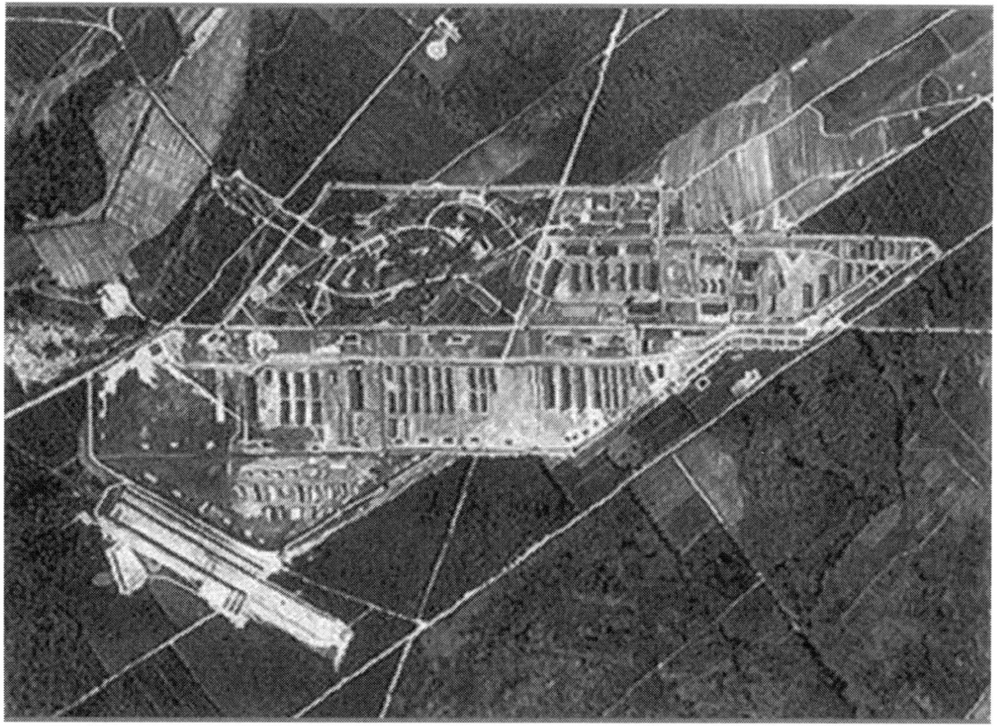

Figure 4. An RAF aerial photo of Bergen-Belsen Camp taken in September 1944. No indication of the conditions inside the camp. Source: Royal Air Force

Figure 5. Vehicles of 63rd Anti-Tank Regiment R.A., part of the advance party directed to take over command of the Bergen-Belsen camp, seen here crossing into the No-Fire Zone. The Germans had erected a notice board 'Danger Typhus' to mark where the Zone started. © Imperial War Museums (BU 3927)

Figure 6. Joseph Kramer, the SS Commandant of Bergen-Belsen Concentration Camp. He met our advance party outside the camp on 15th April. Before he was posted to Belsen, he was at Auschwitz in Poland and was one of the SS who selected arriving prisoners either to join slave work gangs or, if they were not fit enough to work, to be killed in the gas chambers. © Imperial War Museums (BU 3748)

LIBERATING BELSEN CONCENTRATION CAMP

Figure 7. Some of the SS guards were lined up outside the camp when we got there. We were told there had been about 300 SS guards at the camp, but when they learned about the German-British agreement, most of them 'melted away'. Most of the men in this picture had been guards at Auschwitz under Kramer. Source unknown

Figure 8. In addition to the male guards, lined up outside the camp were some 30 female SS guards. Like the male guards, most of these women had arrived with Kramer from Auschwitz. © Australian War Memorial

Figure 9. While talking with Kramer, we heard shooting from within the camp. Lieutenant-Colonel Taylor decided to take Kramer and go inside; I went with them. We were followed by an army loud-hailer truck. We entered the prison camp and drove along this road; it was about half a mile long. We had our first sight of what came to be known as the 'Horror Camp'. There were barbed-wire enclosures and huts on both sides of the road. Some dead bodies are lying at the side of the road. © Imperial War Museums (BU 3768)

Figure 10. A view of one of the perimeter fences. A watch tower in the background. © Imperial War Museums (BU 4711)

Figure 11. The prisoners lined the sides of the road; many seemed too dazed to know what was happening, that we were the British Army come to rescue them. © Imperial War Museums (BU 4006)

Figure 12. Our loud-hailer truck announced, 'You are safe now. The Germans have gone. Food and water will arrive soon. Stay in your huts.' This, of course, to prevent the further spread of typhus. © U.S. Holocaust Memorial Museum, courtesy of Jack and Iris Mitchell Bolton

Figure 13. Barbed wire enclosures sectioned the camp into separate areas. The state of the prisoners started to become apparent. © Imperial War Museums (BU 3764)

Figure 14. As we drove through the camp, we were horrified to see in some of the open areas, piles of corpses—tangled masses of arms and legs. © Imperial War Museums (BU 3755)

Figure 15. In some areas, there were live prisoners next to the corpses, seemingly oblivious of them. © Imperial War Museums (BU 3767)

Figure 16. Amongst some trees we saw hundreds more corpses. After nine months of combat, I had got used to battle casualties, but I had never seen anything approaching what I saw that day. It was unbelievable! Source unknown

Figure 17. Then at the end of the road, we arrived at a large pit partly full of corpses, both men and women — there must have been several hundred. © Imperial War Museums (BU 3777)

Figure 18. When we got back to the camp entrance, Taylor told Kramer and the SS men and women that they were all under arrest and to surrender their arms. Here, the SS are being searched by the British before being confined to their barracks under guard. © Australian War Memorial

LIBERATING BELSEN CONCENTRATION CAMP

Figure 19. The next day, 16th April, the British Army units ordered to the camp by XIII Corps Headquarters started to arrive and reconnoitre. Here, you see them being welcomed by the inmates. Source unknown

Figure 20. I returned to XIII Corps HQ on the evening of 15th April and reported to the Corps Commander what I had seen. The next day, I was instructed to return to the camp and join the Military Government Detachment that had been sent there. I was asked to look into the huts and report what I found. I started with the men's huts. The conditions were beyond appalling. The bunks had three and four men in them, nearly all desperately ill. Most of the men were not much more than skeletons. I went into several huts; the conditions in all of them were about the same: indescribably ghastly. Some of the occupants of the bunks were actually dead. The stench was unbearable. Source unknown

Figure 21. In the women's huts, it was the same. The huts were designed for 80 to 100 inmates—most had over 500 in them. No washing or toilet facilities. © Imperial War Museums (BU 4018)

Figure 22. In several of the women's huts, there were no bunks. Most had over 500 prisoners in them. The prisoners had to sleep on the floor. © Imperial War Museums (BU 4017)

Figure 23. The huts were so crowded that there was not even enough room for any of the women to lie down. © Imperial War Museums (BU 3736)

Figure 24. In one hut I visited, the women were jam packed into a corridor. © Imperial War Museums (BU 3735)

Figure 25. In the weeks before we arrived, nearly every day, several hundred new prisoners had been arriving from other concentration and slave labour camps. To try to cope with the overcrowding, the Germans had turned one area into a 'Women's Tented Camp'. A storm had damaged or destroyed most of the tents but many prisoners were trying to shelter in what was left of them. © Australian War Memorial

Figure 26. In other areas, there were prisoners wandering about aimlessly. The state of the men in this photo was pitiful. Source unknown

LIBERATING BELSEN CONCENTRATION CAMP

Figures 27, 28. Many were obviously starved, just skeletons, very ill indeed. © Imperial War Museums (BU 3766, BU 3728)

Figures 29, 30. Our troops tried to talk with some of the inmates. There were so few of us and tens of thousands of inmates. There was so much to be done that there was very little time for establishing personal relationships. Moreover, language was a major problem. Very few inmates spoke English. © Imperial War Museums (BU 4002, FLM 1226)

LIBERATING BELSEN CONCENTRATION CAMP

Figures 31, 32. There were about 500 children in the camp; they were 'Exchange Jews'. There were several thousand Exchange Jews, including these children, who were being held ready to be exchanged for German civilians interned by the Allies. Very few such exchanges took place. © Imperial War Museums (BU 4111, BU 4108)

Figure 33. See with what indifference this young inmate is walking past many dozens of corpses. For him this was an everyday sight! Photo by George Rodger/The LIFE Picture Collection/Getty Images

Figure 34. There were dead bodies in various stages of decomposition everywhere. These women are carrying away a corpse to put with a large pile of other corpses at the back at the tent.
© Imperial War Museums (BU 3791)

Figure 35. Some other inmates dragging another corpse to join the hundreds of others piled under the trees. © Imperial War Museums (BU 3724)

Figure 36. The same sickening sight everywhere. Kramer told us that in the past few weeks the prisoners had been dying at the rate of 500 a day, faster than they could be buried. He estimated the number of unburied corpses to be about 10,000. A staggering figure! © Imperial War Museums (BU 4029)

Figure 37. Brigadier Glynn-Hughes the senior Medical officer of the 2nd British Army, had arrived and had taken overall charge of the situation. He called a meeting of officers and set out a list of priorities. The two most important and urgent tasks were supplies of water and food. I was detailed to take charge of the distribution of water in the camp and to get the camp's water system working again as soon as possible. The water system had broken down about four days before we arrived and since then there had been no water in the camp for drinking or washing. The only water was in two open tanks built to supply water in case of fire in the camp. The water in those tanks was foul; nevertheless I saw desperate prisoners scooping it up in rusty cans. © Imperial War Museums (BU 3761)

Figure 38. XIII Corps headquarters had detailed the Royal Army Service Corps to divert a number of water carts to Belsen. I established six water points along the camp's road. About twenty men had been allocated to me to keep the prisoners from mobbing the water points and to help those who were too weak to help themselves. We had the carts being emptied and refilled and emptied again till dark. That 'drill' went on from dawn to dusk for the next two or three days. © Danish Army Vehicles

Figure 39. I heard that the Civilian Fire Service in the nearby town of Celle had some portable pumps. The firemen and their pumps were quickly brought to the camp and we started drawing water from a stream that ran along one edge of the camp © Imperial War Museums (BU 4239)

Figure 40. On the day after liberation Royal Army Service Corps trucks arrived with several army cooks and a large number of army Compo ration packs. They quickly prepared a stew from the contents of the Compo packs. © Imperial War Museums (BU 4242)

Figure 41. There had been no food in the camp for several days and distributing the stew to many thousands of starving and desperate inmates and controlling the crowds was a problem. We had nowhere nearly enough soldiers to take this food to each hut and we had to rely on the system the Germans had used. Inmates from each hut had to come to the cookhouse, collect bin-loads of stew and carry them back to their huts. © Photo Archive, Yad Vashem, Jerusalem

LIBERATING BELSEN CONCENTRATION CAMP

Figure 42. Another urgent task was burying the 10,000 corpses lying between and around the huts. It was decided to use the SS guards to pick up the corpses, and place them in trucks for transport up to the end of the camp where the large burial pit was located. © Imperial War Museums (BU 4061)

Figure 43. Here you see the British soldiers supervising the SS in loading up one of the trucks. This dreadful operation went on from dawn to dusk. © Imperial War Museums (BU 4025)

LIBERATING BELSEN CONCENTRATION CAMP

Figure 44. When the trucks arrived at the pit at the end of the camp, other SS would carry the corpses and drop them into the open grave. © Imperial War Museums (BU 4035)

Figure 45. This work did not seem to disturb the SS, but the 'Tommies' were horrified watching those emaciated corpses that had been normal people tossed into a pit like so much rubbish. © Imperial War Museums (BU 4060)

Figures 46,47. The women SS guards were made to handle the corpses too. © Imperial War Museums (BU 4030, BU 4031)

Figure 48. Women SS guards were photographed unloading the dead bodies and dropping them into the pit. © Imperial War Museums (BU 4032)

Figure 49. Some of the piles of corpses were so decomposed that they could not be handled. The army bulldozer that had been brought in was used to dig a pit next to the piles and then simply push the corpses into the pit. Imagine the thoughts of the two young soldiers who took it in turns to drive the bulldozer! © Imperial War Museums (BU 4058)

Figure 50. So that the German civilians could not in the future say 'it never happened,' during these burials we brought the mayors and other prominent German civilians from miles around the camp to the burial sites to witness for themselves what their countrymen had perpetrated on innocent people. Army photographers recorded the scene for future generations. Source unknown

LIBERATING BELSEN CONCENTRATION CAMP

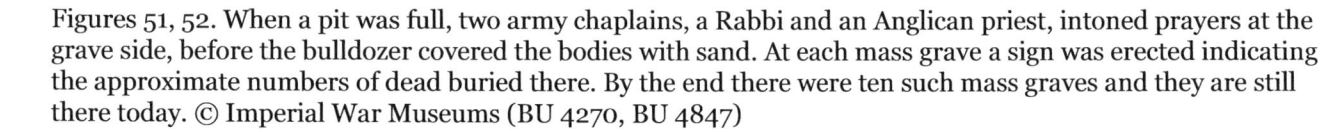

Figures 51, 52. When a pit was full, two army chaplains, a Rabbi and an Anglican priest, intoned prayers at the grave side, before the bulldozer covered the bodies with sand. At each mass grave a sign was erected indicating the approximate numbers of dead buried there. By the end there were ten such mass graves and they are still there today. © Imperial War Museums (BU 4270, BU 4847)

Figure 53. After having organized the water supply, I was given the job of scouring the countryside to find what food stocks there might be that we could requisition. We knew there was a German Army barracks two miles up the road from the concentration camp. I found there a very large military barracks. (The German Army had left several days prior.) This is the entrance. The two-story barrack blocks stretch away in the distance. Source unknown

LIBERATING BELSEN CONCENTRATION CAMP

Figure 54. The Barracks was a Panzer (tank) training school designed for 20,000 soldiers. There were many dormitory buildings, fully equipped with beds and bedding, dining halls and lecture rooms. Under the agreement, the barracks had been emptied of German military. I found the food store of the barrack, holding hundreds of tons of various foodstuffs, tinned meat, powdered milk, vegetables, sugar, cocoa, potatoes etc. I also found there a large bakery capable of baking 60,000 loaves a day, and a stock of many tons of flour. The barracks was requisitioned by our Military Government and work started on converting it into a vast hospital and a Transit and Rehabilitation Camp into which we would evacuate the inmates of the concentration camp. © Imperial War Museums (BU 4705)

Figure 55. The barracks included a 200-bed hospital still with its staff and medical supplies. There were a number of wounded German soldiers still there; arrangements were made for them to be sent to other hospitals. The Panzer Barracks hospital was taken over by a British field hospital and used for sick concentration camp ex-prisoners. Source unknown

Figure 56. Part of the Panzer Barracks was converted into a hospital, and on the sixth day after the liberation, we were able to start evacuating the sick from the concentration camp. Doctors of the Royal Army Medical Corps went into each hut and checked on the state of the men or women inside. They had to decide which of the sick inmates to rescue and move to the Panzer Barracks hospital. They then marked their foreheads with a pencilled cross. The doctors selected those who were sick but saveable—those that were beyond saving were left there to die. © Imperial War Museums (BU 4196)

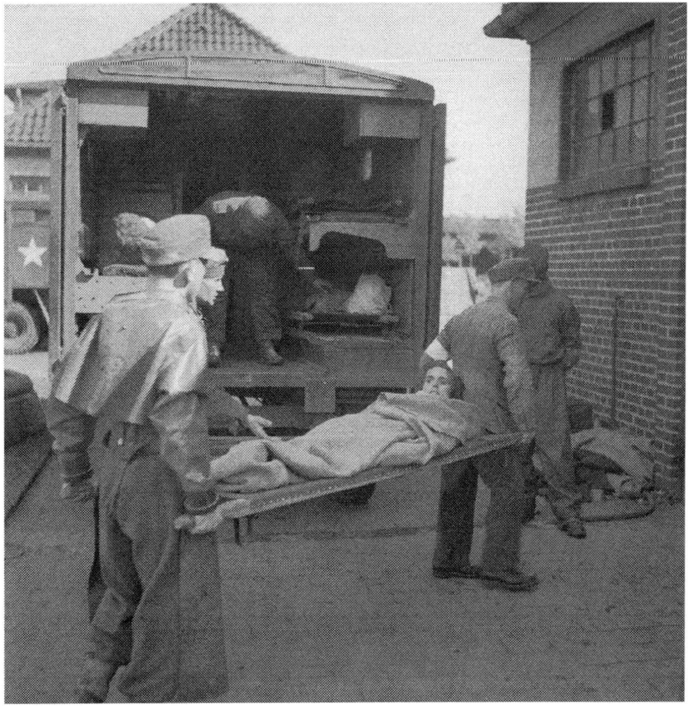

Figure 57. Then stretcher bearers would strip naked those the doctor had selected, wrap him or her in a blanket and stretcher them into the waiting ambulance. The discarded lice-infested clothing was piled outside the hut and destroyed. © Imperial War Museums (BU 4680)

Figures 58, 59. Typhus is carried by lice; the great fear was bringing typhus from the concentration camp into the new hospital we had created. A 'human laundry' was set up in the stables of the barracks—when the sick inmates arrived at the hospital they were thoroughly washed and de-loused before entering the wards. This 'human laundry' was staffed by German Army doctors and nurses transferred from the Panzer Barracks hospital, working under British Army supervision. © Imperial War Museums (BU 5474, BU 5471)

Figure 60. By the time the concentration camp was emptied, between 14,000 and 15,000 patients had been admitted and treated in the hospital created in the barracks—the largest hospital in the world, before or since.
© Photo Archive, Yad Vashem, Jerusalem

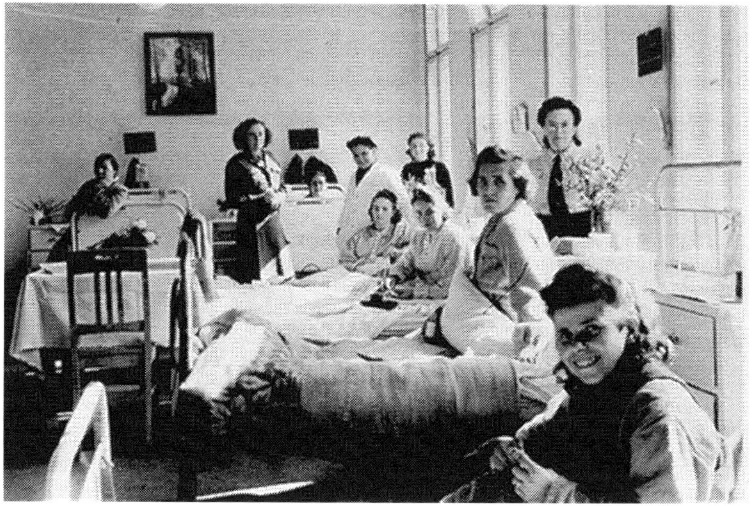

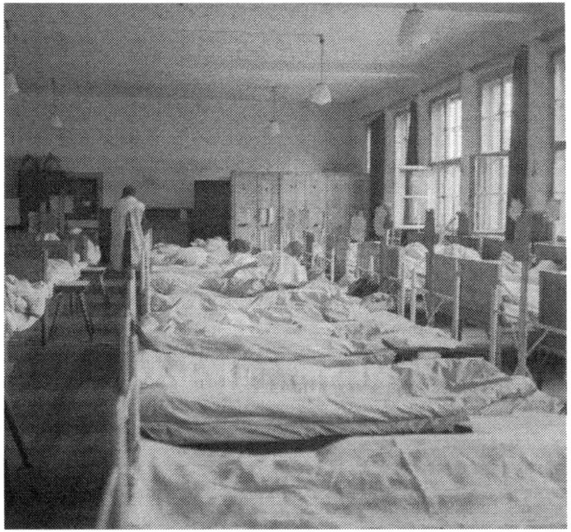

Figures 61, 62. One of the wards of the Panzer Barracks hospital. © US Holocaust Memorial Museum, courtesy of Gedenkstaette Bergen-Belsen, and © Imperial War Museums (BU 5484)

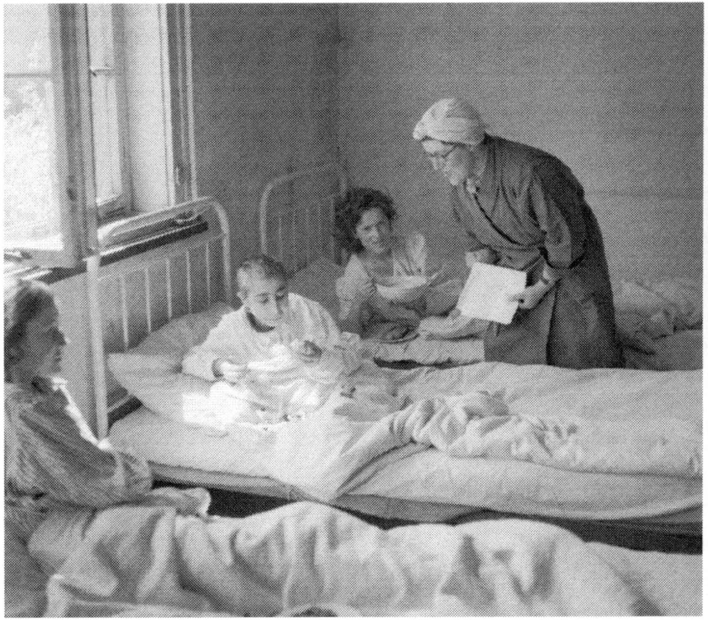

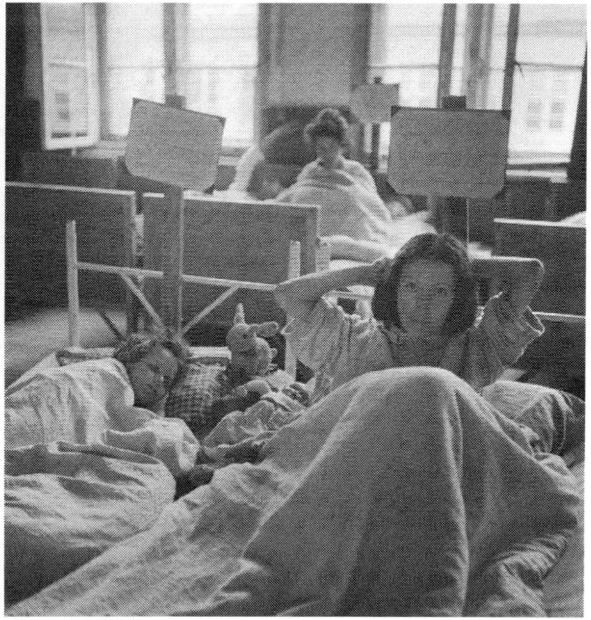

Figures 63, 64. Patients recovering in one of the hospital's many wards. As soon as patients had recovered they were moved to the Transit and Rehabilitation part of the Barracks. © Imperial War Museums (BU 4709, BU 5481)

Figure 65. The ex-prisoners who were classed as 'fit' (if they could walk, they were 'fit') were evacuated from the concentration camp to the Transit and Rehabilitation Camp that was set up in the blocks of the Panzer Barracks. The rest of the blocks were used as the hospital. As soon as the Transit Camp area was ready, evacuation of the so-called fit started. Evacuation was by nationality: the Western Europeans were evacuated first because we knew they would be quickly repatriated, next were Russians and then other nationalities where we knew that repatriation arrangements were planned. First, each ex-prisoner was registered, then given some soap and a towel so they could take a shower.
© Imperial War Museums (BU 5462)

Figure 66. Ex-prisoners taking a warm shower in the showers that the Army Mobile Bath Units had set up. © Imperial War Museums (BU 4237)

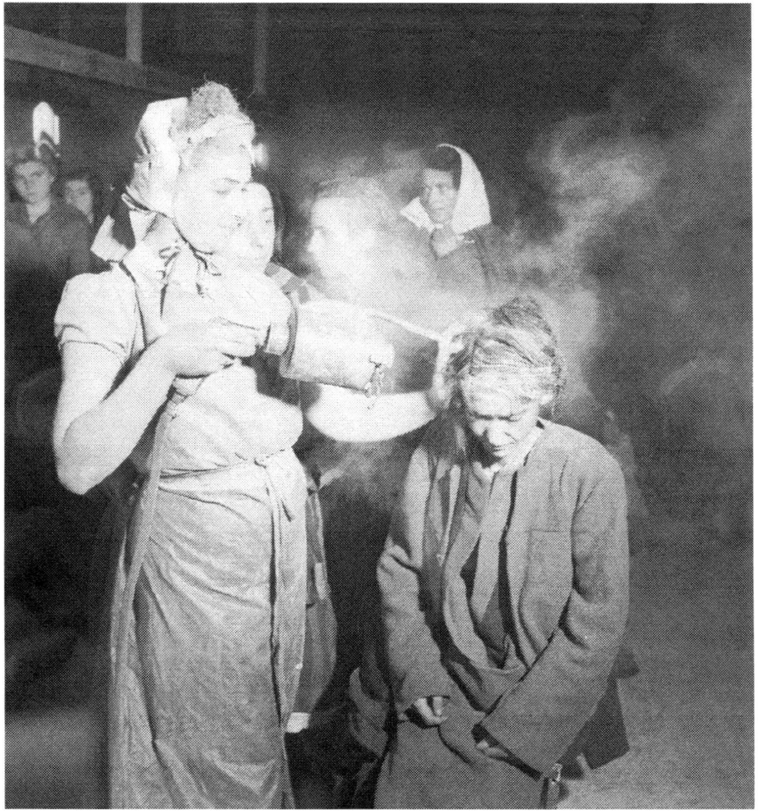

Figure 67. After dressing in clean clothes, the inmates were dusted with DDT powder to kill the lice which spread typhus. Here the dusting is being done by other former camp inmates (many of whom were trained nurses before being interned) under the supervision of the Royal Army Medical Corps. © Imperial War Museums (BU 5467)

Figure 68. Finally, the 'fit' ex-prisoners were helped into trucks to be ferried to the Transit Camp in the Barracks. All of us worked twelve to fourteen hours a day, 'processing' and evacuating 1,000 thousand weak and sick people every day. Even at this rate, it took three weeks to empty the camp. © Imperial War Museums (BU 5469)

Figure 69. Nearly all of the ex-prisoners were underweight and emaciated. One of the most important functions of the Transit and Rehabilitation Camp was to ensure that the inmates received three decent meals a day. This is a scene in one of the dining halls of the Panzer Barracks. © Imperial War Museums (BU 4853)

Figure 70. The Military Government Detachments organized the compulsory donation of clothing and footwear from all the German households, clothing and shoe shops in the surrounding area. In the Transit Camp we set up a clothing centre; every ex-prisoner was given a complete outfit of decent clothing. The media named this centre 'The Harrods of Belsen'!
© Imperial War Museums (BU 6365)

Figure 71. Many of the children were orphans, their mothers having died in the concentration camp. © Photo Archive, Yad Vashem, Jerusalem

Figure 72. With the help of Red Cross workers and teachers among the ex-prisoners, we set up a school for the children. © Imperial War Museums (BU 7801)

Figure 73. As to the concentration camp itself, by 19th May the last inmate had been evacuated and army flamethrowers were brought in to burn down all the more than 100 huts. The last hut was torched on 21st May. The officer in this picture is Brigadier Glynn-Hughes. As the chief medical officer of the British Army in Germany he was in overall charge of the liberation and rescue of the Belsen Concentration Camp. Of the about 50,000 prisoners still alive when we arrived, some 13,000 died in the weeks that followed. As horrific as this number is, without Glynn-Hughes's tireless efforts and organization, the number of deaths would have been even higher. © U.S. Holocaust Memorial Museum

Figure 74. After the concentration camp was burned down and closed, the army erected this notice board near the entrance. © Imperial War Museums (BU 6955)

Figure 75. In September 1945 a War Crimes Trial was convened in Lüneburg, not far from Belsen. There were forty-five defendants. The accused were defended by British Army officers with legal qualifications (seen sitting in front of the accused). Eleven of the forty-five defendants, including Kramer, were found guilty and were hanged. Most of the others were given long gaol sentences. Source unknown

About the Author

Leonard Berney was born in London in 1920. After leaving St Paul's School, Hammersmith in 1938 he joined the Territorial Army as a Second Lieutenant. At the beginning of 1939 he and his Anti-Aircraft Regiment were mobilized for full-time military service in the defence of London. He took part countering The Blitz and the V1 flying bomb attacks. In August 1944 he was in Normandy as the Staff Officer, Anti-Aircraft Defence, of XIII Corps of the British 21st Army.

This is his personal account of his experience of the Liberation of Belsen Concentration Camp and as the Commandant of the Displaced Persons camp that housed the survivors. Following his time at Belsen, he was appointed Military Governor of Schleswig-Holstein and was released from the army at the end of 1946, rank of Lieutenant-Colonel.

He pursued a business career until he retired. Today, Leonard Berney is regularly asked to deliver lectures on the Liberation of Belsen, by groups such as Congregation Ner Tamid, Las Vegas and Greenwich University, London and he is often asked to take part in documentaries on the Holocaust such as *Night Will Fall* which was broadcast on television in twenty countries around the world to mark Holocaust Memorial Day 2015.

Leonard now lives on the residential ship The World. In his

95th year when he wrote this book, he has to be one of the very few survivors of the liberators of the infamous Bergen-Belsen Concentration Camp.

Leonard Berney as a 2nd Lieutenant, aged 18 in 1939 before the outbreak of war.

Appendix
British Army Units Deployed in the Liberation and Rescue Operation

General Duties
Royal Artillery

63rd Anti-Tank Regiment R.A.

113 LAA Regiment R.A.

113 LAA Regiment Workshops R.E.M.E.

172 Battery, 58th LAA Regiment R.A.

174 Battery, 58th LAA Regiment R.A.

Medical
Royal Army Medical Corps

9 (British) General Hospital R.A.M.C.

81 (British) General Hospital R.A.M.C.

29 (British) General Hospital R.A.M.C.

11 Light Field Ambulance R.A.M.C.

163 Field Ambulance R.A.M.C.

32 Casualty Clearing Station R.A.M.C.

35 Casualty Clearing Station R.A.M.C.

7 Field Transfusion Unit R.A.M.C.

22 Field Transfusion Unit R.A.M.C.

30 Field Transfusion Unit R.A.M.C.

30 Field Hygiene Section R.A.M.C.

76 Field Hygiene Section R.A.M.C.

7 Mobile Bacteriological Laboratory R.A.M.C.

Vascular Injuries Research Team R.A.M.C.

Military Government and Control

10 Military Government Garrison Detachment

102 Military Government Control Section

224 Military Government Detachment

618 Military Government Detachment

817 Military Government Detachment

904 Military Government Detachment

908 Military Government Detachment

912 Military Government Detachment

3 Military Government Inland Detachment

12 Displaced Persons Assembly Team

Water and Food Supplies, Transport

Royal Army Service Corps

1575 Light Artillery Platoon R.A.S.C.

1576 Heavy Artillery Platoon R.A.S.C.

404 Company R.A.S.C.

567 Company R.A.S.C.

155 Detail Issue Depot R.A.S.C.

166 Detail Issue Depot R.A.S.C.

Intelligence and Photography

14 Amplifying Unit, Intelligence Corps

317 Field Security Section, Intelligence Corps

No. 5 Army Film and Photographic Unit

No. 1 War Crimes Investigation Team

37 Kinema Section R.A.O.C.

Other Units

102 Mobile Laundry and Bath Unit

104 Mobile Laundry and Bath Unit

314 Mobile Laundry and Bath Unit

6th Airborne Division Mobile Bath Section

8 Corps Mobile Bath Section

11th Armoured Division Mobile Bath Section

15th Scottish Division Mobile Bath Section

35 Pioneer Group, Royal Pioneer Corps

Abbreviations

R.A. – Royal Artillery

R.E.M.E. – Royal Electrical and Mechanical Engineers

R.A.M.C.– Royal Army Medical Corps

L.A.A. – Light Anti-Aircraft

R.A.O.C. – Royal Army Ordinance Corps

T.D. – Territorial Decoration

Printed in Great Britain
by Amazon.co.uk, Ltd.,
Marston Gate.